NATIONAL
GEOGRAPHIC

T0045447

POLES APART

PATHFINDER EDITION

By Dolores Johnson and Michael E. Ruane

CONTENTS

More than 100 years ago, African American explorer Matthew Henson did what no one had ever done before. He braved freezing cold, ice, and racism to reach the North Pole.

ARCTIC

ADVENTURER

By Dolores Johnson

Author of National Geographic's book *Onward*

C

Matthew Henson charged fast across the ice. The **North Pole** was just miles away. It was April 1909, and no one had ever reached the top of Earth before.

Henson carved a path in the ice. The runners of his sled sliced through crusted snow like knives. His dogs howled with excitement as they pulled the sled.

Suddenly, the ice cracked. Henson, his dogs, and the sled plunged into the icy waters of the Arctic Ocean. Henson struggled. He swallowed frigid water. Had he wasted his life chasing a dream, only to fail?

Ice Dangers

Many explorers had tried to reach the North Pole. They faced a brutal maze of dangers. Pressure ridges rose as high as six-story buildings. Deep crevasses, or holes, gaped in the ice. Temperatures dropped as low as minus 50° Celsius (minus 59° Fahrenheit).

That spring, as Henson raced toward the Pole, the ice began its annual thaw. Leads, or watery breaks in the ice, made travel very dangerous. Yet Henson was determined to succeed.

The Journey Begins

Henson's Arctic dream began 18 years earlier with an offer from explorer Robert Peary. The pair had worked together in Nicaragua. Peary was an engineer. Henson began working as Peary's servant. He quickly became his right-hand man.

In 1891, Peary began planning a trip to Greenland, within the **Arctic Circle**. He wanted to use Greenland as a base for a later **expedition** to the North Pole. Peary wanted Henson's help. Yet he wondered if a man whose ancestors came from the warm climate of Africa could survive the cold.

"I'll go North with you, sir, and I think I'll stand it as well as any man," a confident Henson said. Peary agreed. On the trip, Henson built sleds. He also hunted, cooked, and even made crutches when Peary broke his leg.

Both men wanted to be celebrated explorers like Christopher Columbus. Henson thought that if he succeeded, he could help make all African Americans feel proud. At the time, most black people in America held unskilled jobs. They certainly were not expected to become famous, respected explorers.

Rough Going. *Expedition members traveled over steep and jagged ice (below). To stay on top of the snow, they wore special snowshoes (right).*

Survival Skills

In Greenland, expedition members stayed with the native people, the Inuit. Henson learned the Inuit language. He treated them as family. "I have come to love these people," he wrote in a book about his travels. The Inuit called Henson "Maripaluk"—Matthew, the Kind One.

They taught Henson skills needed to survive in the harsh Arctic. He learned how to build icehouses, called igloos. He learned how to hunt caribou and musk oxen.

Inuit women use fox fur and seal and deer skins to sew warm outfits for the explorers. The Inuit also taught the explorers the key to Arctic travel—how to drive dogsleds.

Facing Setbacks

Between 1891 and 1906, Peary led seven trips to the Arctic. Each time, his team learned hard lessons about the dangers there. Sleds broke. Dogs weakened and died. Men got hurt. Peary even lost most of his toes to frostbite.

Ice floated on the ocean below the explorers' feet. It took them miles off course. The ice groaned and creaked. It split apart. They could not cross the watery leads until the ice refroze.

Each trip took Peary and Henson closer to the Pole. They tried reaching the Pole in 1906 but were forced to turn back. Two years later, they decided to try again. They were getting older. This expedition would likely be their last.

On July 6, 1908, Peary, Henson, and six other explorers sailed for Cape Sheridan, Canada. Their ship battered its way through an ocean clogged with icebergs. They landed 665 kilometers (413 miles) south of the North Pole.

The expedition had 19 sleds, 133 dogs, and 24 men, including 17 Inuit. They packed pemmican (sweetened ground meat and animal fat), biscuits, condensed milk, and tea for each man. They brought unsweetened pemmican for the dogs.

Arctic Outfit. *Henson wore a fur suit sewn by Inuit women.*

Tracing His Steps. *This map shows the route Henson followed to reach the North Pole.*

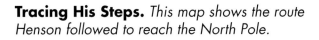

5

Final Assault on the Pole

The final expedition began in late February 1909. "From now on, it was keep on going—and we kept on," Henson wrote. Peary sent a team ahead to carve the trail. They used axes to cut through giant pressure ridges. It was cold. "Our breath was frozen to our hoods," Henson wrote.

As the expedition neared the North Pole, Peary sent most of the men back. Only a small group would make the final push. That way, there would be enough food and supplies. Finally, Peary had sent everyone back except Henson and four Inuit. Henson was overjoyed. He was going with Peary to the North Pole!

By early April, they had only 214 kilometers (133 miles) more to go. Peary sent Henson and his team of Inuit ahead to break the final trail. Yelling, "Huk! Huk!" Henson urged his barking dogs forward. Each day, he drove his sled up to 40 kilometers (25 miles).

All went well, until the moment Henson fell into the water. Henson struggled. Ootah, an Inuit, grabbed him by the collar and pulled him out. Ootah guided Henson's dog team to sturdier ice. Henson was wet and cold. But his dream was still alive.

Farthest North

On April 5, Peary looked through his sextant. The **navigation** tool showed him that the North Pole was only 56 kilometers (35 miles) away! On April 6, Peary once again asked Henson to carve the route north.

He only stopped when his instincts told him he had reached the North Pole. He and his team built igloos. When Peary arrived 45 minutes later, Henson said: "I think I am the first man to sit on top of the world."

Peary's sextant confirmed it. They were within five kilometers (three miles) of the North Pole. That was close enough to claim success. Safe in their igloos, the men fell into an exhausted sleep.

The next day, Peary took the team several miles beyond camp to be sure they actually touched the North Pole.

Bundled Up. *Henson wore this fur suit on his travels. It kept him warm at the icy, cold North Pole.*

Success! *At the North Pole, Henson (center) and four Inuit members of the expedition posed with flags.*

Returning Home

Henson led the way south. After a 16-day dash across the ice, they reached their ship. As they sailed home, they got shocking news. Dr. Frederick Cook was an explorer who'd gone on earlier Peary expeditions. Cook now claimed he had reached the North Pole in 1908—almost a year before Peary and Henson.

Cook was a likable person. The American people believed him. Henson tried to defend the Peary expedition. People laughed at him. They called him ignorant. They didn't believe a black man had reached the North Pole.

An investigation found that Cook had lied. Peary won awards and a special place in history as the first person to reach the North Pole. He was a celebrated explorer.

Honoring Henson

At first, Henson was remembered only as Peary's servant, not as a famous explorer. Back home, he worked as a messenger and as a clerk for the U.S. government.

At the end of his life, Henson's true role finally became widely known. He won a medal from Congress. He went to the White House. He was invited to join the famous Explorers Club. In 2000, after his death, the National Geographic Society gave Henson its highest honor, the gold Hubbard Medal.

Today, the two famous explorers are united forever. Peary and Henson are buried side by side. The words on Henson's tombstone read: "The lure of the Arctic is tugging at my heart. To me, the trail is calling."

WORDWISE

Arctic Circle: area surrounding the North Pole

expedition: a long journey by a group of people to explore an area

navigation: helping by guiding one's way during travel

North Pole: the northernmost point of Earth's axis

South Pole: the southernmost point of Earth's axis

Race to the

Join two explorers as they rac

By Michael E. Ruane

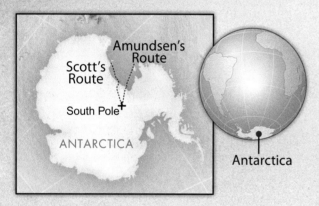

Amundsen's Route
Scott's Route
South Pole
ANTARCTICA

Antarctica

T HE PONY WHINNIED as it plunged through the deep snow. Robert F. Scott watched as the pony struggled to get its footing. It took great effort to pull its leg out of the snow, only to sink back in with the next step. Perhaps Scott had made a mistake by bringing so many ponies instead of sled dogs. The ponies were already having trouble.

It was winter in 1911, and Scott hoped to be the first person to reach the **South Pole**. He had already tried once. On another expedition, Scott and two team members had come close to the Pole but had to turn back. Sled dogs had been little help on that trip. That's why he chose ponies this time.

Two Men, One Goal

Scott wasn't the only one trying to reach the South Pole. Roald Amundsen was there, too. He had lived near the North Pole. There, he learned how to train sled dogs and how to dress for cold weather.

Both men dreamed of reaching the South Pole first because they wanted success for themselves and their countries. Scott was from Great Britain; Amundsen was from Norway.

So the trip to the South Pole would be a race! To reach their goal, they would travel more than 2,900 kilometers (1,800 miles). They would suffer frostbite, snow blindness, and starvation. In the end, only one man would be first. The other would lose his life.

Getting Ready

During the winter, each team stayed at their separate camps. They planned and got ready for their trip to the Pole.

Each team decided to follow a different path. Scott planned to take the same one he had used earlier. Amundsen decided to go through an unmapped area.

South Pole

o the bottom of the world.

With their routes selected, the explorers sent out teams to set up supply stations. They left food and fuel for heat at each one. This way, the explorers wouldn't have to carry everything as they made their way to the Pole.

The food the men packed was not the most tasty. Yet it gave them the energy they needed as they tried to reach their goal.

Danger on the Ice

With their last supply station set up, Scott and his team headed back to camp. Then something unexpected happened.

An entire team of sled dogs fell into a deep crack in the ice called a crevasse. Tied together, they now dangled from the edge of the ice.

The frightened dogs yelped. They struggled to free themselves. Slowly, the men pulled them to safety. Two dogs had come free from the harness. They had fallen onto a ledge below the surface. They were trapped.

A rescue attempt seemed too risky. Yet Scott refused to leave the dogs behind. He ordered his men to use a rope to lower him down to the ledge. He scooped up the dogs. Then the men hauled Scott and the dogs to safety.

Better Equipment. *A member of Amundsen's team works on a sled to make it slide easily on ice and snow.*

Working Dog. *Chris was one of the few sled dogs that Scott used on his trip to the South Pole.*

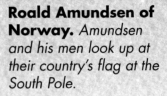

Roald Amundsen of Norway. *Amundsen and his men look up at their country's flag at the South Pole.*

The Race Begins

AMUNDSEN: Finally, spring came. At last, Amundsen felt ready. He chose his four toughest men to go with him. Once they loaded the sleds, the dogs sped off, and the men skied beside them.

Snow and bitter winds pushed against them. Wearing reindeer furs kept the men warm. Sealskin boots kept their feet dry.

Amundsen and his men worked well as a team. One day, a howling blizzard roared across the ice. In less than an hour, the team calmly set up their tents, fixed a meal, and fed the dogs.

SCOTT: Meanwhile, Scott was still in his camp. He finally set out two weeks after Amundsen. He still believed the ponies were hardier than sled dogs. If the ponies or dogs failed him, Scott planned to have his men pull the sleds themselves.

Shortly after setting out, Scott's men were already feeling the cold. Their clothes were mostly made of wool. Once wet, the clothing took a long time to dry. The men often complained of feeling damp and cold.

AMUNDSEN: Weeks passed. Amundsen's dogs were growing thin from all the hard work. The men were hungry, too. Some of them were getting frostbite on their fingers and toes.

Now, a large glacier stood in their path. The tired dogs fought to pull the sleds up the steep ice. They dug their claws deep into the ice to keep their footing. Each step was a struggle. They pressed on for days.

SCOTT: Scott and his men were falling farther behind. Another blizzard struck. The men knew it was too dangerous to lead the ponies through the storm. Scott and his men stayed in their tent to wait it out.

Outside, the ponies sunk to their bellies in new, wet snow.

The storm lasted for four days. The ponies did not survive. Now Scott and his men had to pull the sleds themselves.

AMUNDSEN: Amundsen's men were still hungry and suffering from frostbite. The dogs were eating anything left unguarded. They even tried to eat a pair of boots!

Then one afternoon, Amundsen stopped the sleds. He checked his navigation instruments. Then he told his men that they were standing at the South Pole.

The men could not believe they were the first to reach the Pole. They marked the Pole with the flag of Norway. They left a tent with some supplies and a note for Scott.

SCOTT: While Amundsen was at the Pole, Scott and his men continued to haul their sleds. They were growing sick and weak. Weeks passed.

One morning, Scott saw something in the distance. It was the flag that Amundsen had left behind as a marker. Scott's heart sank because he knew he had lost the race.

His team reached the Pole 34 days after Amundsen. They were disappointed. They did not stay long. Scott and his team began the long march back. Each step was a struggle. A blizzard struck, and they could not go on.

Non-slip Shoes. *Scott's men wore shoes with spikes to help them walk on the ice.*

Recovery Mission

Months later, a rescue party found Scott's tent. He and his teammates had died of starvation and extreme cold.

Throughout the expedition, Scott had kept a journal. In it, he wrote everything that had happened. Amundsen did the same.

We retell their stories to inspire others. Their incredible journeys led to further study of this untamed part of the world, and that journey continues. Today's explorers go to the farthest reaches of our planet and beyond to make amazing discoveries.

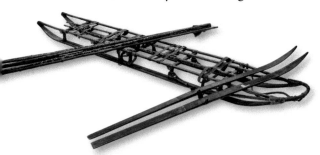

Real Gear. *Scott's team used these skis and sled.*

Reach Your Goals

Join the race to the Poles and answer
these questions.

1 What skills did Henson learn from
the Inuit?

2 How did Henson contribute to his
expedition's success?

3 Why were Scott and Amundsen in
a race to reach the South Pole?

4 How were Scott's and Amundsen's
preparations for their trips the
same? How were the preparations
different?

5 What two questions do you have
about the trips to the Poles?
Where can you look to
find the answers?